Word Bird's

What Does Word Bird See?

Published in the United States of America by The Child's World®, Inc.
PO Box 326
Chanhassen, MN 55317-0326
800-599-READ
www.childsworld.com

Project Manager Mary Berendes
Editor Katherine Stevenson, Ph.D.
Designer Ian Butterworth

Library of Congress Cataloging-in-Publication Data
Moncure, Jane Belk.
What does Word Bird see? / by Jane Belk Moncure.
p. cm.
Summary: Word Bird sees animals and insects in their
unique homes, from beavers and mice to ants and bees.
ISBN 1-56766-993-X (lib. : alk. paper)
[1. Animals—Fiction. 2. Insects—Fiction.]   I. Title.
PZ7.M739 Whb 2002
[E]—dc21
2001006039

Word Bird's

What Does Word Bird™ See?

by Jane Belk Moncure
illustrated by Chris McEwan

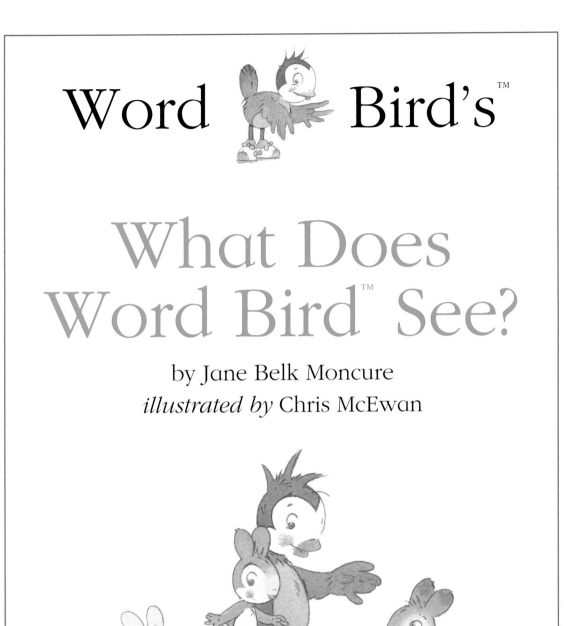

Word Bird sees. . .

a hole in
a tree.

Who lives there?

Squirrels.

"Hi, squirrels."

Word Bird sees . . .

a hole in
the grass.

Who lives there?

Rabbits.

"Hi, rabbits."

Word Bird sees . . .

a hole in the house.

Who lives there?

A mouse.

"Hi, mouse."

Word Bird sees. . .

a house made of sticks.

Who lives there?

A beaver.

"Hi, beaver."

Word Bird sees . . .

a hole in a mound.

Who lives there?

Ants.

"Hi, ants."

Word Bird sees. . .

a pretty shell.

Who lives there?

A turtle.

"Hi, turtle."

Word Bird sees. . .

a funny shape.

Who lives there?

Bees!

"Bye-bye, bees."

Can you read these words with Word Bird?

tree

hole

mound

ants

squirrel

shell

grass

turtle

rabbit

funny shape

house

mouse

sticks

bees

beaver

bye-bye